W9-AUE-482

OAKWOOD ES MEDIA
940 OAK MANOR DR
GLEN BURNIE   MD

00264242480

MY FIRST JOKES AND RIDDLES

# Why Do Elephants Wear Purple Suspenders?

OAKWOOD ES MEDIA
330 OAK MANOR DR
GLEN BURNIE MD

## by Judy Ziegler

GALLERY BOOKS
An Imprint of W. H. Smith Publishers Inc.
112 Madison Avenue
New York City 10016

A wish has been granted

To *Oakwood ES*

From *Christopher Kohlway*

Scholastic Book Fairs®

## An RGA Book

Copyright © 1991 by RGA Publishing Group, Inc.
This edition published in 1991 by Gallery Books,
an imprint of W.H. Smith Publishers, Inc., 112 Madison Avenue,
New York, New York 10016
Manufactured in the United States of America
Gallery Books are available for bulk purchase for sales promotions
and premium use. For details write or telephone the Manager of
Special Sales, W.H. Smith Publishers, Inc., 112 Madison Avenue,
New York, New York 10016. (212) 532-6600

ISBN 0-8317-6297-7

# Why didn't the leopards take the bus to school?

They couldn't get it through the door.

3

# How did the bear make the hot dog shiver?

He covered it with chilly beans.

# What's a musical bug?

A humbug.

What do you call an otter who shaves 50 times a day?

Did you hear about the hyena who was banging his head on the piano keys?

He was playing by ear.

# What do you call two banana skins?

A pair of slippers.

# Why did the turkey eat so fast?

He was a gobbler.

# Where do rabbits catch the bus?

At the bus hop.

# Why did the mongoose wear his shirt in the bath?

The label said wash and wear.

13

# What's the best way to catch a fish?

Have it thrown to you.

# What do apes sing at Christmas?

„Jungle bells, Jungle bells…"

# Why didn't five cats under one umbrella get wet?

It wasn't raining.

# What is a bull doing when he closes his eyes?

Bull-dozing.

# What do you call a train loaded with gum?

A chew-chew train.

# How do you make a bandstand?

Take away their chairs.

# What makes more noise than a pig stuck in a tree?

*Three pigs stuck in a tree.*

# Why did the zebra plant birdseed?

24

He wanted to grow parakeets.

What did the eagle say when he got a new comb?

"Cawww! Cawww!"

What happened to the white rabbit when he jumped in the Red Sea?

He got wet.

# What do you do with a blue gila monster?

Cheer him up!

# What does a polar bear eat?

Iceburgers.

# What ballet do pigs love most?

*Swine Lake.*

# What's brown and turns cartwheels?

A pony pulling a cart.